Little People, **BIG DREAMS**™

MARIA MONTESSORI

Written by
Maria Isabel Sánchez Vegara

Illustrated by
Raquel Martín

Frances Lincoln
Children's Books

Little Maria was born in Italy with an incredible will to learn. Her parents thought that, one day, she could become a great teacher.

But her school was the most dull and boring place on Earth. So, Maria invented games to make learning more fun.

When Maria finished elementary school, she was eager to study science. But this was not encouraged for girls, so she had to go to an all-boys technical school.

Maria decided to become a doctor. Despite all the obstacles in her way, she made it to college. She was the first girl in Italy to study medicine.

She was not allowed to be in the same room as the other students when there was a body to examine, and had to study it alone once the class was over. But Maria didn't give up!

Once she graduated, Maria became an assistant doctor in a mental health clinic, where disabled children were treated as if they were sick. Their only toys were the breadcrumbs left from breakfast.

So Maria decided to give the children love and respect as part of their treatment. She knew that in order to give their best, all the children needed was to believe in themselves.

And she was right! By using games and fun activities, the children started to learn through play. Maria realized her idea could work with any child.

She opened a school called the Children's House,
where children became their own teachers, and desks
became small tables full of counting beads and puzzles.

Maria was the first person to use cutout letters to teach children how to read. She told her pupils travel stories to make geography fun, and insect tales to explain the natural world.

She wrote many books and articles, and traveled the world giving courses and lectures. She helped hundreds of other teachers use her revolutionary method.

Soon, models of the Children's House sprang up all over the world. Many schools, orphanages, and nurseries followed in her footsteps—from Italy to America and India.

Little Maria inspired children to be free, curious, and responsible human beings. For the children of today are the makers of tomorrow.

MARIA MONTESSORI

(Born 1870 • Died 1952)

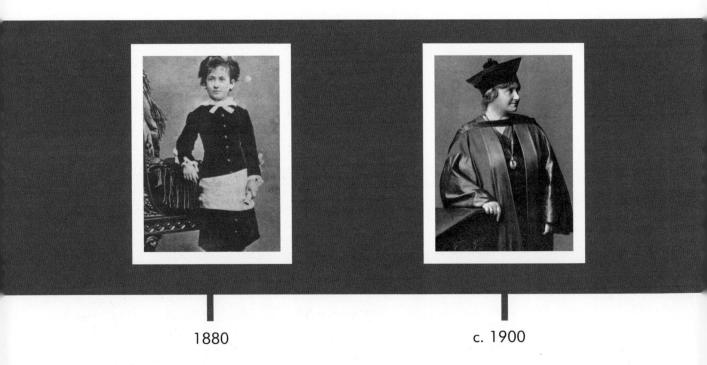

1880

c. 1900

Maria Montessori was born in a town called Chiaravalle, in Italy. Soon
after, her parents moved to Rome so Maria could go to a better school.
At that time in Italy, there were very strict ideas about what girls and boys
should study—and it was not thought that a girl should study science. But
Maria was a trailblazer from the very beginning. She studied math and
science at an all-boys school. Then she decided to become a doctor. She
was the first woman in Italy to go to medical school, so she had a lot of
boundaries to break down in order to be treated equally. Maria studied
hard and specialized in the care of children and mental health. As a newly
qualified doctor, she became known for her support of women's rights and
famous for her respect for patients from all backgrounds. She proved that

c. 1907   c. 1930

women could become talented doctors—a revolutionary idea at the time. Maria's work then took her to a mental health hospital, where she worked with children who had learning disabilities. She noticed that the children were deprived of toys and activities. She thought that if they received special education and care, they would start to flourish. She began to research and try out this idea, with great results. The children started to learn. She then took it a step further: Maria proved that all children could become their own teachers, if they were given engaging activities and freedom to explore. With her revolutionary ideas and respectful attitude, Maria transformed the education system. Even though she died in 1952, the legacy of her work continues today in Montessori schools around the world.

Want to find out more about **Maria Montessori?**
Read one of these great books:

Maria Montessori and Her Quiet Revolution by Nancy Bach and Leo Latti
Our Peaceful Classroom by Aline D. Wolf and Montessori School Children
You may have even gone to a Montessori school!

Brimming with creative inspiration, how-to projects, and useful information to enrich your everyday life, Quarto Knows is a favorite destination for those pursuing their interests and passions. Visit our site and dig deeper with our books into your area of interest: Quarto Creates, Quarto Cooks, Quarto Homes, Quarto Lives, Quarto Drives, Quarto Explores, Quarto Gifts, or Quarto Kids.

Text copyright © 2019 Maria Isabel Sánchez Vegara. Illustrations copyright © 2019 Raquel Martín.
Original concept of the series by Maria Isabel Sánchez Vegara, published by Alba Editorial, s.l.u
Produced under trademark licence from Alba Editorial s.l.u and Beautifool Couple S.L.

First Published in the USA in 2019 by Frances Lincoln Children's Books, an imprint of The Quarto Group.
100 Cummings Center, Suite 265D, Beverly, MA 01915, USA.
T +1 978-282-9590 **www.QuartoKnows.com**

First Published in Spain in 2019 under the title Pequeña & Grande Maria Montessori
by Alba Editorial, s.l.u., Baixada de Sant Miquel, 1, 08002 Barcelona
www.albaeditorial.es
All rights reserved.

ISBN 978-1-78603-755-8
The illustrations were created in gouache.
Set in Futura BT.

Published by Rachel Williams • Designed by Karissa Santos
Edited by Katy Flint • Production by Jenny Cundill

Manufactured in Guangdong, China CC112020

Photographic acknowledgements (pages 28–29, from left to right) 1. Maria Montessori age 10, 1880 © The Maria Montessori Archives held at Association Montessori Internationale, Amsterdam 2. Maria Montessori in academic gown, c.1900 © Hulton Archive / Stringer via Getty Images 3. Maria Montessori and child in the classroom, c. 1907 © ullstein bild Dtl. via Getty Images 4. Maria Montessori, c. 1930 © ullstein bild via Getty Images

Collect the *Little People*, **BIG DREAMS**™ series:

FRIDA KAHLO

ISBN: 978-1-84780-783-0

COCO CHANEL

ISBN: 978-1-84780-784-7

MAYA ANGELOU

ISBN: 978-1-84780-889-9

AMELIA EARHART

ISBN: 978-1-84780-888-2

AGATHA CHRISTIE

ISBN: 978-1-84780-960-5

MARIE CURIE

ISBN: 978-1-84780-962-9

ROSA PARKS

ISBN: 978-1-78603-018-4

AUDREY HEPBURN

ISBN: 978-1-78603-053-5

EMMELINE PANKHURST

ISBN: 978-1-78603-020-7

ELLA FITZGERALD

ISBN: 978-1-78603-087-0

ADA LOVELACE

ISBN: 978-1-78603-076-4

JANE AUSTEN

ISBN: 978-1-78603-120-4

GEORGIA O'KEEFFE

ISBN: 978-1-78603-122-8

HARRIET TUBMAN

ISBN: 978-1-78603-227-0

ANNE FRANK

ISBN: 978-1-78603-229-4

MOTHER TERESA

ISBN: 978-1-78603-230-0

JOSEPHINE BAKER

ISBN: 978-1-78603-228-7

L. M. MONTGOMERY

ISBN: 978-1-78603-233-1

JANE GOODALL

ISBN: 978-1-78603-231-7

SIMONE DE BEAUVOIR

ISBN: 978-1-78603-232-4

MUHAMMAD ALI

ISBN: 978-1-78603-331-4

STEPHEN HAWKING

ISBN: 978-1-78603-333-8

MARIA MONTESSORI

ISBN: 978-1-78603-755-8

VIVIENNE WESTWOOD

ISBN: 978-1-78603-757-2

MAHATMA GANDHI

ISBN: 978-1-78603-787-9

DAVID BOWIE

ISBN: 978-1-78603-332-1

WILMA RUDOLPH

ISBN: 978-1-78603-751-0

DOLLY PARTON

ISBN: 978-1-78603-760-2

BRUCE LEE

ISBN: 978-1-78603-789-3

RUDOLF NUREYEV

ISBN: 978-1-78603-791-6

ZAHA HADID

ISBN: 978-1-78603-745-9

MARY SHELLEY

ISBN: 978-1-78603-748-0

MARTIN LUTHER KING JR.

ISBN: 978-0-7112-4567-9

DAVID ATTENBOROUGH

ISBN: 978-0-7112-4564-8

ASTRID LINDGREN

ISBN: 978-0-7112-5217-2

EVONNE GOOLAGONG

ISBN: 978-0-7112-4586-0

BOB DYLAN

ISBN: 978-0-7112-4675-1

ALAN TURING

ISBN: 978-0-7112-4678-2

BILLIE JEAN KING

ISBN: 978-0-7112-4693-5

GRETA THUNBERG

ISBN: 978-0-7112-5645-3

JESSE OWENS

ISBN: 978-0-7112-4583-9

JEAN-MICHEL BASQUIAT

ISBN: 978-0-7112-4580-8

ARETHA FRANKLIN

ISBN: 978-0-7112-4686-7

CORAZON AQUINO

ISBN: 978-0-7112-4684-3

PELÉ

ISBN: 978-0-7112-4573-0

ERNEST SHACKLETON

ISBN: 978-0-7112-4571-6

STEVE JOBS

ISBN: 978-0-7112-4577-8

AYRTON SENNA

ISBN: 978-0-7112-4672-0

LOUISE BOURGEOIS

ISBN: 978-0-7112-4690-4

ELTON JOHN

ISBN: 978-0-7112-5840-2

JOHN LENNON

ISBN: 978-0-7112-5767-2

PRINCE

ISBN: 978-0-7112-5439-8

CHARLES DARWIN

ISBN: 978-0-7112-5771-9

CAPTAIN TOM MOORE

ISBN: 978-0-7112-6209-6

HANS CHRISTIAN ANDERSEN

ISBN: 978-0-7112-5934-8

STEVIE WONDER

ISBN: 978-0-7112-5775-7

MEGAN RAPINOE

ISBN: 978-0-7112-5783-2

MARY ANNING

ISBN: 978-0-7112-5554-8

MALALA YOUSAFZAI
ISBN: 978-0-7112-5904-1

ACTIVITY BOOKS

STICKER ACTIVITY BOOK

ISBN: 978-0-7112-6012-2

COLORING BOOK

ISBN: 978-0-7112-6136-5

LITTLE ME, BIG DREAMS JOURNAL

ISBN: 978-0-7112-4889-2